HELPING YOURSELF
HELPING OTHER

Dealing with

SCHOOL
SHOOTINGS

Kate Shoup

Cavendish
Square

New York

C000196685

Published in 2020 by Cavendish Square Publishing, LLC
243 5th Avenue, Suite 136, New York, NY 10016

First Edition

Website: cavendishsq.com

This publication represents the opinions and views of the author based on his or her personal experience, knowledge, and research. The information in this book serves as a general guide only. The author and publisher have used their best efforts in preparing this book and disclaim liability rising directly or indirectly from the use and application of this book.

All websites were available and accurate when this book was sent to press.

Library of Congress Cataloging-in-Publication Data

Names: Shoup, Kate, 1972- author.
Title: Dealing with school shootings / Kate Shoup.
Description: First edition. | New York : Cavendish Square, 2020. |
Series: Helping yourself, helping others | Includes bibliographical references and index. |
Audience: Grades: 7-12. Identifiers: LCCN 2018053872 (print) | LCCN 2019001075 (ebook) |
ISBN 9781502646316 (ebook) | ISBN 9781502646309 (library bound) | ISBN 9781502646293 (pbk.)
Subjects: LCSH: School shootings--Juvenile literature. | School shootings--Prevention--Juvenile literature.
Classification: LCC LB3013.3 (ebook) | LCC LB3013.3 .S5 2020 (print) | DDC 371.7/82--dc23
LC record available at https://lccn.loc.gov/2018053872

Editorial Director: David McNamara
Editor: Caitlyn Miller
Copy Editor: Rebecca Rohan
Associate Art Director: Alan Sliwinski
Designer: Ginny Kemmerer
Production Coordinator: Karol Szymczuk
Photo Research: J8 Media

The photographs in this book are used by permission and through the courtesy of:
Cover Dot Art/Shutterstock.com; p.4 Steven D Starr/Corbis Historical/Getty Images; p. 11 Vincent Kline/Getty Images; p. 12 Stephen B. Goodwin/Shutterstock.com; p. 15 Katherine Welles/Shutterstock.com; p. 23 Toshifumi Kitamura/AFP/Getty Images; p. 25 Puttawat Santiyothin/Shutterstock.com; p. 28 Joseph Sohm/Shutterstock.com; p. 34 (people in photos are models and the images are being used for illustrative purposes only) Michaeljung/Shutterstock.com; p. 39 (people in photos are models and the images are being used for illustrative purposes only) AJ_Watt/E+/Getty Images; p. 42 (people in photos are models and the images are being used for illustrative purposes only) Hero Images/Getty Images; pp. 44, 68, 78 ©AP Images; p. 47 Miami Herald/Tribune News Service/Getty Images; p. 51 Ringo Chu/AFP/Getty Images; p. 59 Jim Watson/AFP/Getty Images; p. 60 Mark Makela/Corbis News/Getty Images; p. 64 David McNew/Hulton Archive/Getty Images; p. 73 Mandel Ngan/AFP/Getty Images; p. 75 John Moore/Getty Images; pp. 80, 89 Chip Somodevilla/Getty Images; p. 82 (people in photos are models and the images are being used for illustrative purposes only) Antonio Guillem/Shutterstock.com; p. 86 Denver Post/Getty Images; p. 90 Maria Savenko/Shutterstock.com; p. 95 Jeffrey J Snyder/Shutterstock.com; p. 98 Pool/Getty Images; p. 100 (people in photos are models and the images are being used for illustrative purposes only) Monkey Business Images/Shutterstock.com; Background (sidebar) Mika Besfamilnaya/Shutterstock.com.

Printed in the United States of America

Some of the images in this book illustrate individuals who are models.
The depictions do not imply actual situations or events.

CONTENTS

RIGHT LANE
MUST
TURN RIGHT

Chapter 1

School Shootings in America

On the morning of April 20, 1999, Eric Harris and Dylan Klebold—both seniors at Columbine High School near Littleton, Colorado—launched one of the deadliest school shootings in American history. At 11:19 a.m., Harris and Klebold, wearing black trench coats that concealed multiple guns, began shooting on school grounds. During the next forty-nine minutes, the boys murdered twelve of their fellow students and one teacher, and wounded twenty-one others. They also set off several

Opposite: Students flee Columbine High School during a shooting that killed twelve students and one teacher.

pipe bombs, set the cafeteria on fire, shot up the principal's office, and traded gunfire with police. Finally, at 12:08 p.m., as law-enforcement officers closed in, Harris and Klebold took their own lives. As devastating as this attack was, it might have been even worse: Harris and Klebold had placed more than one hundred explosive devices throughout the school, intending to cause even greater harm. Thankfully, most of these failed to go off.

There were warning signs. Harris posted threatening messages online, and Klebold wrote disturbing stories. The two allegedly showed classmates the weapons they were collecting. In the wake of the Columbine shooting, American schools would change the way they handled students who threatened violence.

SCHOOL SHOOTINGS: BY THE NUMBERS

The Centers for Disease Control and Prevention (CDC) is the US government agency responsible for protecting public health. It used to be that the CDC did a lot of research on the effects of guns on public health. In a 1993 study on gun ownership, the agency found that, on the whole, keeping a gun in the home did not protect people from harm. In fact, it made it almost three times more likely that someone inside the home—usually a friend or family member—would be shot and killed.

Pro-gun groups like the National Rifle Association (NRA) worried that the findings of this and other reports on gun use would cause the public to push for controls on gun ownership. To prevent this, these groups lobbied US lawmakers to ban the CDC from speaking in favor of gun control. They also convinced lawmakers to withdraw funding for CDC research on guns. Lawmakers enacted this policy in 1996. Since then, the CDC has conducted no research on gun violence in the United States, including school shootings. (Interestingly, the lawmaker behind this policy, Republican congressman Jay Dickey, later regretted its enactment. He even joined with

Mark Rosenberg, who had been responsible for overseeing research on gun violence at the CDC before Congress shut it down, to push for increased funding for gun research.)

Today, the CDC maintains databases on all sorts of public-health problems, such as infectious diseases, drug use, and automobile accidents. These databases help researchers track these problems and come up with ways to possibly solve them. No such CDC database exists for gun violence or school shootings, however. This makes it extremely difficult to determine exactly how many school shootings have occurred in the United States, and to solve the problem of gun violence in schools.

Complicating matters, different groups define school shootings in different ways. For example, the *Washington Post* defines a school shooting as any shooting that occurs on school grounds at an elementary or a secondary school immediately before, during, or after the school day. Using that definition, as of October 2018, there have been

221 shootings since 1999. At least 141 students, teachers, and staff have been killed, and an additional 287 people wounded.

Others use a wider definition. For example, the Gun Violence Archive, which is a nonprofit organization that tracks gun violence, defines school shootings the same way as the *Washington Post*. But it also includes shootings on college and university campuses, as well as shootings on school property during extracurricular activities such as football games and school dances. As a result, as of October 2018, the Gun Violence Archive cites somewhat larger numbers of school shootings nationwide: 254 since just 2012, with 138 killed and 454 wounded.

Sometimes it feels like there's a new school shooting in America every day. In reality, however, school shootings are very rare. The *Washington Post* says the odds of a student being shot to death at school are 1 in 614,000,000. In other words, kids have a better chance of winning the lottery than of being shot at school! Even more rare are so-called school rampages, like the one at Columbine, which involve the random killing of multiple students. As of 2018, just eleven schools have experienced school rampages (defined as a school shooting involving four or more victims and at least two deaths) since 1999.

Still, even one school shooting is one too many. School shootings have a devastating impact not just on the school but on the surrounding community and the nation as a whole. A report by the Federal Bureau of Investigation (FBI) puts it this way: "A tragedy such as the Columbine High School shooting spreads horror, shock, and fear to every corner of the country."

MAJOR ATTACKS IN THE UNITED STATES

Columbine was not the first school shooting in the United States. In fact, a tragic incident in 1840 in which a student at the University of Virginia shot and killed his law professor was the first. Still, Columbine was a chilling turning point. Since Columbine, it sometimes seems like school shootings have become common in America.

The deadliest school shooting in the United States occurred on April 16, 2007, at Virginia Tech University in Blacksburg, Virginia. In that attack, a student named Cho Seung-Hui murdered two students in a dormitory. He then moved to a second building, in which classes were conducted.

The deadliest school shooting in US history took place at Virginia Tech University. The shooter killed twenty-seven students and five faculty members before taking his own life. Here, a police officer walks in front of the dormitory where two students were killed during the attack.

The Texas Tower Sniper

More than forty years before Cho Seung-Hui's rampage at Virginia Tech, another devastating mass shooting occurred on an American college campus: at the University of Texas at Austin, on August 1, 1966.

The man who committed this mass shooting was twenty-five-year-old Charles Whitman. Whitman had earned a scholarship to the university in 1961 but lost it two years later due to poor grades. Perhaps this was

The Texas tower sniper took aim from the observation platform at the top of this building.

what motivated Whitman— who had also been a Marine sharpshooter and was known to struggle with violent impulses— to haul an arsenal of weapons and more than seven hundred rounds of ammunition to the observation deck high atop a building on campus and open fire.

In all, Whitman murdered seventeen people: his wife and mother, whom he had stabbed earlier that morning; three people inside the building below the observation deck; and an additional twelve on the ground, including one unborn baby. He also wounded thirty-one others. The rampage, which lasted more than ninety minutes, ended when two law-enforcement officers cornered Whitman on the observation deck and shot him dead.

Interestingly, after Whitman's death, an autopsy revealed a small tumor on the part of the brain that controls emotion. Investigators concluded this tumor might have had something to do with Whitman's frequent violent behavior.

Cho fired into several classrooms, killing thirty and wounding seventeen, before turning one of his two semiautomatic pistols on himself.

A particularly heartbreaking school shooting occurred on December 14, 2012, at Sandy Hook Elementary School in Newtown, Connecticut. That attack began when a twenty-year-old former student named Adam Lanza, dressed in black fatigues and a military vest and armed with a semiautomatic rifle and two pistols, shot through a glass panel by the school's locked main doors to gain entrance. The school principal, psychologist, and lead teacher quickly confronted Lanza. He shot all three. One survived. Lanza then walked into a first-grade classroom, where he killed a substitute teacher, a behavioral therapist, and fifteen children. In another first-grade classroom, Lanza killed a teacher, a teacher's aide, and five more children. As police closed in on the scene, Lanza, who had also murdered his mother before attacking the school, took his own life. (Since the shooting, some fringe members of society have claimed it was a hoax. There is absolutely no evidence to support this claim, which has done real and lasting harm to family members of those murdered in the attack.)

More recently, a school shooting at Marjory Stoneman Douglas High School in Parkland, Florida, on February 14, 2018, left fourteen students and three staff members dead, and seventeen others wounded. In this attack, a nineteen-year-old former student named Nikolas Cruz, armed with a semiautomatic rifle and several rounds of ammunition, entered

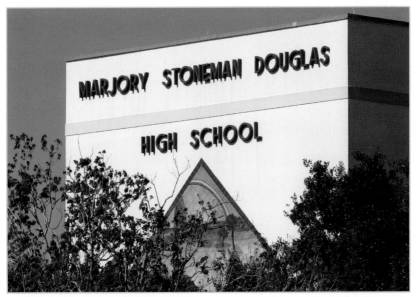

Marjory Stoneman Douglas High School in Parkland, Florida, was the site of a deadly school shooting.

the building, set off a fire alarm, and, as teachers and students flooded from their classrooms, began shooting. Unlike Harris, Klebold, Cho, Lanza, and many other school shooters, Cruz did not take his own life. Instead, he set down his rifle and left the scene. He was arrested by police just over an hour later.

SHOOTINGS AROUND THE WORLD

Although most school shootings take place in the United States, they have occurred elsewhere around the world. For example, in March 1996, a gunman murdered sixteen children and one teacher, and wounded ten others, at an elementary school in Scotland. A year later, a gunman in Yemen murdered six children and two adults at two separate schools.

Canada has experienced multiple shootings. Three of these occurred in Montreal. The first was at the École Polytechnique in 1989, in which a gunman murdered fourteen women and injured ten more.

(Four men were also injured in the attack.) The second was in 1992, at Concordia University, where a staff member murdered four colleagues. The third was at Dawson College in 2006. That shooting left one student dead and more than a dozen wounded.

Germany has also experienced multiple school shootings. In 2000, a student gunman killed a teacher in Branneburg. Two years later, in Erfurt, an expelled student murdered thirteen teachers, two students, and one policeman. In 2009, in Winnenden, a former student murdered nine students and three teachers, a gardener at a neighboring psychiatric hospital, and a salesperson and customer at a nearby car dealership.

School shootings have also occurred in Sweden (2001) and Finland (2008), in Argentina (2004) and Brazil (2011), and elsewhere.

Still, school shootings are arguably an American phenomenon. Between 2000 and 2010, the United States experienced twenty-seven school shootings—just one fewer than thirty-six other countries *combined*. In the first five months of 2018, more than twice as many people were killed in school shootings in the United States (twenty-seven) as military members on active deployment (thirteen).

CAUSES FOR SCHOOL SHOOTINGS

There is no single cause for school shootings. This type of violent behavior is very complex. However, researchers have identified many possible contributors to these events.

The most commonly cited contributors are bullying, mental illness, exposure to violent content, family dynamics, traumatic loss, and easy access to guns. Often, a particular school shooting will occur because of a combination of these contributors.

Several researchers cite bullying as a contributor to school shootings. A 2002 report issued by the US Secret Service and the US Department of Education, called the "Safe School Initiative" (SSI) report, noted that almost three-quarters of school shooters felt "persecuted, bullied, threatened, attacked, or injured by others prior to the incident."

In many cases, this bullying—perhaps better described as torment—was ongoing and severe. In one case, said the report, "nearly every child in the school had at some point thrown the attacker against a locker, tripped him in the hall, held his head under water in the pool, or thrown things at him." Sadly, social media has amplified the effects of bullying. All too many young people find themselves the victim of online gossip or rumors, teasing, and other hostile interactions.

One particular form of bullying seems to be especially damaging: the kind meant to emasculate. Research shows that some school shooters, who are overwhelmingly male, were mocked for being gay (whether they were or not). Others were taunted for having "unmanly" physical traits—for example, being scrawny or short. For these boys, guns become an equalizer. In fact, kids who have been bullied are reportedly five times more likely to carry a weapon than kids who haven't.

Another contributor to school shootings may be mental illness. Recent shootings support this claim. The Sandy Hook shooter was diagnosed with various psychiatric disorders, including anxiety and obsessive-compulsive disorder. Some believe he may also have been schizophrenic. These conditions went untreated, however. The Virginia Tech shooter was declared mentally ill by a Virginia judge. However, researchers say that only one-fifth of school shooters had been diagnosed with a mental disorder—although 61 percent of school shooters had experienced severe depression, and 78 percent had considered suicide prior to the attack.

Separate from mental illness, but related somewhat, are three personality traits that may contribute to violent behavior like school shootings. One is psychopathy. Psychopaths disregard and even violate the rights of others. Heartless and detached, they care only about reaching their own goals, and they don't mind whom they hurt in the process. Indeed, they may not even view other people as human beings. Another trait is narcissism. Narcissists have excessive self-esteem. They feel entitled to extra attention and special treatment, and they lash out when they don't get it. The third trait is Machiavellianism. People who are Machiavellian seek power by any means necessary, including manipulation and even violence. An important report on youth violence, "Youth Violence: What We Know and What We Need to Know," was written by researchers after the Sandy Hook shooting. It notes that having one of these traits is bad enough. However, someone with all three is likely to "embody the lack of empathy, sense of entitlement, and motivation to gain power that appear to facilitate involvement in violence"— like school shootings.

Here are other personality traits that might contribute to school shootings:

- Low self-esteem
- Low tolerance for frustration

- An inability to cope with criticism, rejection, and humiliation

- A lack of resiliency

- A tendency to nurse resentments or deflect blame

- Intolerance toward people of other races, religions, or types

- A suspicious nature

- An inappropriate sense of humor

- Excessive anger

Some researchers view exposure to violent content—including video games, movies, videos, music, and books—as yet another contributor to school shootings. Others dispute this claim based on insufficient evidence. But while there might not be enough evidence to directly link exposure to violent content with school shootings, there *is* sufficient data to link exposure to violent content with increased aggression. Aggression may in turn be a contributing

Playing violent video games could contribute to aggressive and even violent behavior.

factor to school shootings. This could be amplified if a student's friends share a fascination with this type of content.

Family dynamics almost certainly play a role in school shootings. According to the "Youth Violence" report, dynamics such as "harsh and rejecting parents, interparental violence, child abuse and neglect, chaotic family life, inconsistent discipline, and poor monitoring by parents of children showing early signs of aggression" can all contribute to youth violence, including school shootings. The same goes for a family dynamic in which the child "rules the roost." In this scenario, traditional family roles are reversed. As the FBI describes it, "the child acts as if he were the authority figure, while the parents act as if they were the children." Some of these children don't recognize limits, which may cause them to act violently.

Finally, a traumatic personal loss can spark a school shooting. Examples of losses might include the death of a loved one, a divorce in the family, a debilitating illness, or even a painful breakup. Experts believe that nearly all past school shooters experienced such a loss before the attack.

Of course, no shooting can occur without access to a gun. Indeed, easy access to guns is often cited as *the* key contributor to school shootings. A recent study revealed that Americans own more than 393 million guns. That's more guns than there are people in the United States. Some school shooters acquire their weapons by buying them themselves, sometimes illegally. Most, however, find them right at home or get them from friends or relatives. Many of these guns are handguns. In some cases, semiautomatic

Automatic weapons, semiautomatic weapons, and easy-to-conceal handguns make it easy for shooters to cause maximum carnage.

rifles that have high-capacity magazines and are set up for rapid fire are used to cause even more carnage.

It's important to note that just because a student has been bullied, suffers from mental illness or has certain concerning personality traits, consumes violent content, has an unstable family, has suffered a traumatic loss, or has easy access to guns doesn't mean that he or she is likely to carry out a school shooting. Many students are affected by one or even all of these contributors and would never dream of committing an act of violence.

MOTIVES

Just as there are several contributors to school shootings, a shooter might have several motives. According to the SSI report, more than half of all school shooters (61 percent) act out of revenge, often for being bullied or humiliated. Thirty-four percent conducted the shooting to solve some sort of problem, 27 percent out of a feeling of desperation or to attempt suicide, and 24 percent to attract attention. In most cases, a combination of motives drove the shooter to act.

Eighty-one percent of shooters were also motivated by a specific grievance at the time of the attack—perhaps against a teacher or other faculty member or another student, or even the school as a whole. The report defined "grievance" as "a belief that some other person or organization is directly or indirectly responsible for injury or harm to self and/ or someone whom the subject cares about."

Often, the person or people associated with this grievance became a target of the attack. The report notes that this type of targeted attack is far more common than an attack that simply involves random killing. (Still, non-targeted victims might get caught up in the violence.)

WARNING SIGNS

Because there is no school-shooter profile, and millions of students experience one or more contributors associated with school shootings, it can

The Secret Service Takes On School Shootings

In 1999, after Columbine, the US Department of Education partnered with the US Secret Service to study the thinking, planning, and behaviors of school shooters and to identify ways to prevent future attacks.

A 1999 report released by the US Department of State and the US Secret Service has helped authorities as they try to prevent future school shootings.

The Secret Service might seem like a strange partner for this project. After all, its primary function is to protect key figures in the government, such as the president and vice president of the United States and their families. But the agency achieves this in part by identifying, assessing, and containing threats, such as gunmen intent on causing harm. This makes the agency a good fit for the task of predicting and preventing school shootings.

The two agencies issued their findings in 2002 in a report called the "Safe School Initiative" report. Although this report is nearly two decades old, its findings remain relevant today. It serves as an important guide for communities, schools, and students to combat school shootings.

be hard to identify a potential shooter before a violent incident. Still, there are some key warning signs.

The FBI provides examples of concerning behaviors. These include (but are not limited to):

- An unwillingness to resolve a grievance nonviolently

- Engaging in negative interpersonal relations

- Throwing temper tantrums

- Brooding or sulking

- Showing a diminished ability to cope with stressors or setbacks

- Earning poor grades at school

- Isolating oneself from others or withdrawing from activities one enjoys

- A dramatic change in appearance

- Fixating on violence or engaging in violent fantasies

- Fixating on historical or religious figures associated with violence and destruction (such as Hitler or Satan)

- An increasing sense of recklessness
- A diminishing fear of consequences

School shooters rarely just "snap." Most school shootings are planned events rather than impulsive actions. Some shooters take weeks or months to plan, while others take only a few days. Other concerning behaviors, therefore, revolve around planning and preparing for an attack. These might include casing the target area, testing site security, stockpiling weapons, practicing using weapons, accumulating tactical gear, writing a manifesto or producing a video to explain the reasons behind the attack, and staging the attack.

Another warning sign is revealing violent plans to at least one other person, either deliberately or by mistake. This is often called "signaling" or "leakage." For example, the shooter might leak his desire to act violently to a schoolmate. He could submit a class assignment such as a report or a poem that reveals a growing fascination with violent acts. The FBI says, "Leakage is considered to be one of the most important clues that may precede an adolescent's violent act."

Often, the shooter signals his or her plan to at least one peer, such as a sibling, schoolmate, or friend. Indeed, this happens in more than 80 percent of attacks. In some cases, the signal was vague. That is, other people might have been told that something bad was about to happen, but did not know exactly what, where, or when. In other cases, other people had more details, or even contributed to the attack by goading the shooter on, helping the shooter get weapons, or aiding the shooter with planning. Rarely did the shooter's peers inform an adult of the danger.

In very few cases, school shooters issue an explicit threat. The threat could be spoken or written. It could be expressed with a gesture, such as pointing and "shooting" at another person with one's finger or drawing one's finger across one's throat. Figuring out how serious a threat is can be quite difficult. This is why all threats should be reported to an adult, like a teacher or a parent. It's not your responsibility to decide how serious a threat might be, but it is your responsibility to tell someone if you are concerned that a classmate may become violent.

Chapter 2

Preventing School Shootings

*a*fter each new school shooting, calls to prevent them grow louder. But predicting and preventing this type of violence is hard to do. An FBI report on the issue outlines the problem:

> Reliably predicting any type of violence is extremely difficult. Predicting that an individual who has never acted out violently in the past will do so in the future is still more difficult. Seeking to predict acts that occur as rarely as school shootings is almost impossible.

Opposite: Having a culture of respect and trust between students and teachers is one key way to prevent school violence.

This is simple statistical logic: when the incidence of any form of violence is very low and a very large number of people have identifiable risk factors, there is no reliable way to pick out from that large group the very few who will actually commit the violent act.

That being said, researchers *have* identified strategies to prevent some, if not all, school shootings. Some of these strategies involve addressing the main contributors to school shootings. Others center around increasing security in schools. Everyone can play a role in executing these strategies, including communities, health-care providers, schools, families, and students.

ADDRESSING THE MAIN CONTRIBUTORS TO SCHOOL SHOOTINGS

The main contributors to school shootings are bullying, mental illness and concerning personality traits, exposure to violent content, family dynamics, traumatic loss, and easy access to guns. Researchers have identified several strategies to address each of these contributors.

Experts observe that teachers and school staff play a critical role in preventing bullying. To prevent bullying, educators must build a supportive school environment where students feel safe to talk to each other and to staff, and in which there is mutual trust and respect between students and staff.

In addition to reducing bullying, this type of school environment increases the chances that a student will report a potential threat to an adult. Another way to increase the chances that a student will report a potential threat is to establish an anonymous tip line. Schools can also get wind of a prospective shooter's plans by monitoring social media.

Conducting standard mental health and behavioral screenings and providing mental health care to students with emotional or behavioral problems or who have suffered a traumatic loss can also help prevent school shootings. Ideally, these screenings should be handled by mental-health counselors who work in the school. These counselors can then refer students to mental-health professionals outside the school for treatment. Schools can also teach students to develop self-control, manage anger, increase empathy, solve problems, resolve conflict, and cope with rejection and disappointment. This will help improve students' general mindset.

Parents have an important role to play in limiting kids' exposure to violent media. One way to do this is to use a filtering device to restrict violent content on TV or to change computer settings to prevent kids from accessing this kind of content online. Of course, given how much violent content exists, it may be impossible for parents to shield their kids from all of it. Still, parents can help kids put what violent content they do see into context—for example, bringing up other ways of solving conflict besides violence.

Parents can also work to improve family dynamics. Kids whose parents are harsh, abusive, neglectful, or generally disengaged are at a higher risk for aggressive or violent behavior. Kids who live in a chaotic home or receive inconsistent discipline are also at a higher risk. Some parents may need special training to improve family dynamics.

Finally, research suggests that reducing kids' access to guns can help to prevent school shootings. Researchers have noted that weapons besides guns can be used in fatal attacks. However, experts

Improving family dynamics can help to prevent school shootings.

point out that shootings often take the lives of many more people than attacks that involve other weapons. Moreover, guns can be used from a greater distance. Psychologists say that this physical distance can prevent a shooter from seeing victims as real people. Outlawing certain kinds of guns or accessories that make it easier for a gunman to shoot several bullets very quickly without reloading might also help to reduce school shootings—particularly rampage shootings.

Some of these solutions are controversial. For example, many pro-gun groups, such as the NRA, argue that access to guns is not a problem. They also contend that attempts to limit access to guns will not deter a committed attacker. Finally, they claim these solutions go against the Second Amendment to the US Constitution, which guarantees all Americans the right to bear arms. Meanwhile, some health professionals caution against an overemphasis on mental health in solving school shootings. They believe that emphasizing mental health's role in school shootings could stigmatize students who struggle with their mental health and prevent them from asking for help. Clearly, a combination of solutions that address the various aspects of school shootings is needed.

USING HARD SECURITY MEASURES TO PREVENT SCHOOL SHOOTINGS

"Soft" measures to combat school shootings, like the ones just described, may not be enough. Many people want "hard" security measures to prevent school shootings or to protect as many teachers and students as possible if a shooting occurs.

Some hard measures involve securing the school building or grounds. For example, schools might put up fences to protect school grounds from intruders, install metal detectors at school entrances to prevent someone from sneaking a gun inside, lock doors when school is in session to keep intruders out, install locks on classroom doors that can be locked from

The Myth of the "Shooter Profile"

No single "profile" describes a school shooter.

Data reveals that nearly all school shooters are males, most are white, and most are current or former students at the school in question. Beyond that, school shooters share few characteristics.

For example, school shooters come from families of all types. Some attackers had excellent grades— in fact, most attackers did— while others were failing. While a few attackers had no close friends, others were considered mainstream— even popular. Some shooters had been troublemakers prior to the attack; far more had been model students. Only a few had a criminal record or a reputation for committing violence.

For this reason, it's not effective to use profiling to identify school shooters. Most students who fit a so-called school-shooter profile do not pose a risk, while students who don't fit the profile might.

the inside, and replace windows with bulletproof glass. Some schools might go even farther: installing cameras to track intruders who enter the building, systems that detect when a gun is fired, or bulletproof "safe rooms" in classrooms.

A student walks through a metal detector on her way into school.

Other hard security measures have to do with personnel, such as armed security guards or school resource officers. These staff members could serve as a first line of defense if a student opens fire. Their presence might make a potential shooter think twice before carrying out an attack in the first place. Security officers can play other roles too: acting as trusted adults to whom students can go, and as a model for resolving conflicts.

Some schools have even considered arming teachers. Like a security guard or school resource officer, an armed teacher could serve both as a deterrent and a first line of defense against a school shooter. Or instead of arming teachers with guns, schools might equip them with pepper spray to stop a shooter in their tracks. Yet another option might be to equip teachers with a wearable "panic button." Pushing the button puts the whole school on lockdown and notifies law enforcement of an emergency.

Equipping teachers with panic buttons might not prevent a shooting, but it might help limit the casualties if one occurs. So, too, might conducting drills for students and staff to prepare them for a school shooting. There are two main types of drills: lockdown drills and active-shooter drills. In a lockdown drill, teachers lock the classroom door, turn out the lights, gather students in a far corner of the room, and instruct them to be still and quiet until the drill is over. In an active-shooter drill, school officials simulate a school shooting. Sometimes, they even use fake blood and shoot blanks to make the drill seem more like real life. In these drills, teachers might instruct students to escape the building, barricade the door with furniture and hide, or fight the "shooter."

Like the soft measures discussed earlier, some of these hard measures are controversial. For example, putting up fences and metal detectors to secure the building can make a school seem more like a prison. This doesn't help foster the supportive school environment needed to head off school shootings.

Having armed security officers on site may also be a problem. In some instances, security officers *have* deterred or cut short an attack. However, in others—like at Columbine and Parkland—security officers at the scene had little or no effect. More than once, school security officers have discharged their weapons when not faced with a school shooter.

Some schools simulate an active-shooter situation to prepare students for a school shooting.

Sometimes this was on purpose, and sometimes it was by accident. This creates a danger of a different kind.

Arming teachers is even more controversial. While some teachers support this measure, most do not. Many say it would make schools *less* safe. In other words, while arming teachers might help in the unlikely event of a school shooting, it would introduce a new set of potentially more deadly problems, including teachers accidentally setting off their firearm and schoolchildren gaining access to a teacher's gun. Many members of law enforcement also oppose this measure, arguing that more guns on site might result in more chaos during a shooting.

Even drills have their opponents—particularly active-shooter drills. Those opposed say these drills may be traumatizing for students. There is research to back up this claim. For example, a 2018 report issued by the Giffords Law Center to Prevent Gun Violence states that these drills "foster fear and anxiety" and can "intensify the fear of gun violence children already suffer."

ASSESSING A THREAT

All threats are not created equal. Some threats present a clear and real danger; others are likely all talk. "Neither should be ignored," says the FBI. "But reacting to both in the same manner is ineffective and self-defeating." One must assess a threat before deciding how to respond.

The FBI identifies four types of threats. The first type is a direct threat. This type of threat "identifies a specific act against a specific target and is delivered in a straightforward, clear, and explicit manner." An example of a direct threat might be, "I'm going to shoot Mr. Smith in the parking lot after school." The second type of threat is an indirect threat. These threats are less straightforward. They don't identify a specific act or target. For example, "I could kill everyone in this school if I felt like it" is an indirect threat. The third type of threat, called a veiled threat, suggests but does not outright threaten violence, as in, "Everyone would be better off if Tyler weren't around anymore." Finally, a conditional threat is one that warns of a violent act *if* some other event occurs (or doesn't)—for example, "If I get expelled, I'm coming back here with a gun."

The FBI also identifies three levels of threats. These levels are based on the type of threat and the chances that the person who made the threat can or will carry it out. The first type of threat is a low-level threat. Low-level threats are indirect, vague, and implausible, and pose little risk to others. The second type is a medium-level threat. In addition to being more direct and concrete, medium-level threats *could* be carried out, but it's not terribly likely that they will. Plus, there's no sign that the person who made the threat has taken steps to actually act on it. Finally, there are high-level threats. This type of threat is direct, specific, and plausible, and "appears to pose an imminent and serious danger to the safety of others." High-level threats almost always call for immediate action by law enforcement. The FBI summarizes its approach to the different types and levels of threats as follows: "In general, the more direct and detailed a threat is, the more serious the risk of its being acted on."

School officials should use the FBI's approach or something similar when evaluating threats made by students. They should also adopt the FBI's stance that different types of threats require different types

School safety officers can help to assess threats.

of responses. Many schools maintain a zero-tolerance policy for verbal threats of violence regardless of type or level. The result is that students who pose no real risk to the school wind up being suspended or even expelled. This "can undermine positive school climates, marginalizing already challenged children, even propelling them on a trajectory toward prison," says the "Youth Violence" report. That being said, school officials should *never* allow possession of a weapon on school grounds.

HOW STUDENTS CAN PREPARE FOR THE WORST

While school shootings might seem common, the odds of one happening at your school are very low. Still, students can and should take concrete steps to prepare themselves for a school shooting. Here are some ideas:

- Know your way around: Uncover shortcuts and alternate routes in your school. This knowledge might come in handy in the event of a school shooting.

- Identify all exits: Find out where the nearest exit is for each of your classrooms. If you're on a lower floor, your best way out might be a window. Practice opening the window ahead of time. (Ask your teacher for permission first!)

- Locate hiding places: If it's not safe to exit during a shooting incident, you might need to hide. Scope out good hiding places throughout your school—

on school grounds, in the gym and cafeteria, in hallways, and in your classrooms. Look for janitor's closets that can be locked from the inside, large objects you can hide behind, or furniture such as cabinets that you can climb inside.

- Locate potential barricades: Identify pieces of furniture that could be moved in front of a classroom or closet door to prevent a shooter from getting inside. These might include file cabinets, tables, desks, and chairs.

- Look for "weapons": Identify objects to throw at a shooter if he or she makes it inside the classroom. This could distract a shooter or even injure him or her, giving you time to escape. Textbooks, backpacks, scissors, water bottles, and chairs are good options. So is a fire extinguisher. Don't throw the extinguisher, though. Instead, spray its contents at the attacker's eyes and mouth.

- Take a self-defense class: If you can, learn some basic self-defense moves. That way, if you have to fight off a shooter, you'll be prepared.

- Learn first aid: It may take first responders a few minutes to arrive on the scene of a school shooting. If you are unhurt, you can use your own first-aid skills to help nearby teachers or students who have been wounded in the shooting until first responders arrive. You might save someone's life!

- Practice staying calm: In any emergency, including a school shooting, it's critical to stay calm. Practice keeping your cool in other stressful situations by taking deep breaths or using other methods that work for you.

- Ask if your school has a plan in place: Ask a teacher or administrator if your school has a plan in place to respond to a school shooting. If not, ask if you can help create one.

- CReate a plan with your family: Decide how you'll get in touch during or after an emergency, such as a school shooting, and where to meet up after the danger passes.

WHAT TO DO IF YOU GET CAUGHT IN THE CROSSFIRE

Experts used to tell teachers and students to hide in the event of a school shooting. But after Sandy Hook, in which twenty young students and four classroom workers were killed while trying to hide from a shooter, all that has changed. Now experts urge teachers and students to run, hide, or fight, depending on the situation.

The best option, assuming you have a safe escape route, is to run. Drop everything and get away from the shooter. Help others escape if you can. When you're safe, call 911. If you can't run—maybe the shooter is in the hallway outside your classroom and is obstructing your only way out—then your best option is to hide. Lock and block the door, close the blinds, turn out the lights, and get out of view. If you're part of a group, spread out to make things more difficult for the shooter. Be silent. Turn off the ringer on your phone, and make sure it won't vibrate. Text or use social media to communicate with first responders and tag your location to make it easier for them to find you. (You can also put a sign in the window.) Stay in place until the police tell you it's safe to move.

As an absolute last resort, when no other option is available—for example, the attacker has found your hiding place—you should fight ... and fight hard. Be as aggressive as possible. Ambush him or her with whatever weapon you can find. Remember: spraying an attacker's eyes and mouth with a fire extinguisher could be a good way to stop him or her. Then tackle the shooter, take the weapon, and restrain him or her using whatever you have on hand, such as a belt.

During or after a shooting, you might need to tend to wounded teachers or students while waiting for first responders to arrive (assuming that you are not injured yourself). Most likely this will involve trying to control their bleeding. To do so, apply direct pressure to wounded areas. If a tourniquet is called for, and you know to apply one, then do so. You might not have access to a first-aid kit that contains a tourniquet. In that case, you can make one yourself. Tear off a long strip of fabric from your shirt that's 2 to 3 inches (5 to 7.5 centimeters) wide, wrap it above the wound, and use a rod-shaped object or ruler to twist it tight. If people are unconscious, turn them on their side, and keep them warm—perhaps covering them with a coat or sweater.

When first responders arrive, obey all instructions. Keep your hands visible at all times. Do not be alarmed if police have guns or other weapons or if they use tear gas or pepper spray. Their first priority is to gain control of the situation and end the violence, perhaps by shooting and even killing the attacker.

Never Again

After the school shooting at Marjory Stoneman Douglas High School in Parkland, Florida, in which a gunman murdered fourteen students and three staff members, survivors formed a political action committee (PAC) called Never Again MSD with the goal of tightening gun laws and preventing future school shootings.

As part of this effort, the group organized a march on Washington called March for Our Lives, which took place in March 2018. It became one of the biggest protests led by young people in America since the Vietnam War during the 1960s. Organizers estimate that approximately eight hundred thousand people took part. Members of Never Again MSD have also worked hard to raise awareness about political candidates running for office who support legislation to toughen gun laws and to push people to vote.

Not everyone agrees with the efforts of the Parkland survivors. Some pro-gun opponents have even accused them of lying about being at the school during the shooting and called them "crisis actors." There is no evidence to support these accusations.

Parkland survivors and other activists during the 2018 March for Our Lives in Washington, DC

Chapter 3

The Aftermath of School Shootings

*a*ccording to the *Washington Post,* as of October 2018, "more than 215,000 students have experienced gun violence at school since Columbine." That's more than the total population of some entire American cities, like Tacoma, Washington (population 213,418), or Salt Lake City, Utah (200,544). Sadly, each and every one of these students will suffer effects from this traumatic experience all their lives.

Opposite: Mourners gather at a makeshift memorial for the victims of the 2012 Sandy Hook school shooting.

School shootings aren't just traumatic for students. They may also have a devastating effect on:

- Teachers and other staff
- Parents and other family members
- First responders called to the scene
- Medical staff at hospitals who care for the wounded
- Students at nearby schools

Indeed, in the aftermath of a school shooting, the whole community suffers. Even people outside the community may be affected by a school shooting—especially if it results in multiple casualties. When a school shooting like the ones at Columbine, Virginia Tech, Sandy Hook, or Stoneman Douglas occurs, the whole nation—often the whole world—responds with fear, shock, anger, and sadness.

EXPERIENCING A SCHOOL SHOOTING: WHAT IT FEELS LIKE

Many survivors of school shootings have bravely shared their experiences with others. What follows are stories and quotes from several of these survivors. (Some of these stories and quotes may be upsetting to read.)

For many students who have experienced a school shooting, the first hint of trouble was the sound of gunfire. That was true for Brooke Harrison at Marjory Stoneman Douglas High School in Parkland, Florida, who wrote of the shooting there: "Then I heard it: BANG! BANG! BANG!" Colin Goddard had a similar experience during the shooting at Virginia Tech. "We heard these loud bangs coming from outside the building," he later recalled. "At first, they were muffled and distant … [then] they were much louder and much closer."

Following the shooting, these Columbine students bravely spoke about their experiences.

Often, students were initially confused by the sound. "I didn't realize what they were at first," said Paige Curry of the gunshots she heard during a 2018 shooting at Santa Fe High School in Santa Fe, Texas. The same was true for Jordan Laudanno during the Marjory Stoneman Douglas shooting. "At the time, we didn't think anything of it," she recalled afterward. "Because why would you think there [were] gunshots going on in your school?"

Some students assumed the shots were part of a drill. Others supposed they were a joke. That was the case for Columbine survivor Melissa Miller. "I thought it had to be a firecracker—some kind of senior prank," she wrote. Even when Miller saw the shooters holding rifles on the school steps outside, she figured they were just paintball guns.

For most, however, the danger quickly became clear. "I realized what [the gunshots] were when we heard screaming," Paige Curry told a reporter. For Melissa Miller, it was when the shooters opened fire. "Bullets struck students on the sidewalk, in the parking lot, and on the hill," she recalls. "That's what made me realize—oh, my God!—it was no joke."

Faced with a school shooting, teachers, staff, and students were forced to decide whether to run, hide, or fight. Emily Mayberry, who survived a shooting at Northern Illinois University in 2008, ran. "I just knew I wanted to get away from campus," she said later. "I ran for a total of two miles before I stopped. I just kept running."

More often, students were forced to hide. That was the case for Alfonso Calderon at Marjory Stoneman Douglas. "Our teacher told us to get into the closet in the back of the room," Calderon said during an interview after the shooting. Melissa Martin took cover behind a car in the school parking lot. "I quickly ducked behind a white truck," she wrote. "I did not dare look up … I was scared to move an inch." Many terrified students, including Jordan Laudanno, called or texted their parents while in hiding. "I didn't want to freak [my mother] out," Laudanno said. "But I wanted to say 'I love you.' Just in case."

Some students who hid were lucky; the gunman never found them. Others were less fortunate. Virginia Tech survivor Colin Goddard recalled finding himself face-to-face with the shooter: "My first thought was, 'This must be a cop who heard us and climbed into the building to help us.' And then I saw him turn down a row of desks, and I realized I was wrong."

Moments later, Goddard was shot. "All of a sudden, I felt like I had been kicked as hard as you can imagine above the right knee," he said. "It was a burning, stinging, sharp pain. I went numb and then felt warmth down my leg." The gunman also shot Goddard above his hip and in his right armpit.

Many students who escaped physical injury suffered a trauma of another type: watching their friends or teachers be gunned down—some even killed. Brooke Harrison of Marjory Stoneman Douglas wrote of witnessing the death of one of her best friends: "Not a single second goes by where I don't think about her and dread the truth that I'm never seeing her again."

On rare occasions, students or teachers were able to fight back when confronted with the shooter. During a shooting at Seattle Pacific University in 2014, a student named Jon Meis "got pepper spray from my backpack and sprayed [the shooter] in the face twice." He then tackled the shooter, disarmed him, and, with the help of another student, held him down until police arrived. In another shooting, in Noblesville, Indiana, in 2018, seventh-grade science teacher Jason Seaman tackled the shooter, suffering three gunshot wounds in the process. "My actions on that day ... were the only acceptable actions I could have done given the circumstances," Seaman said afterward. "I care deeply about my students and their well-being. That is why I did what I did that day."

Seventh-grade teacher Jason Seaman was shot when he tackled the shooter during an attack in Noblesville, Indiana.

For most students, the nightmare ended only when help arrived. But even that sometimes proved traumatizing. When the SWAT team came for Jordan Laudanno and her schoolmates at Marjory Stoneman Douglas, "We all thought we were going to die right then and there," she said. "They yelled, 'everyone get on the floor, put your hands in the air' … They were screaming at us … They had their guns pointed at us to make sure the shooter wasn't in the room and that none of us had weapons." The SWAT team then led Laudanno and her classmates outside, warning them to keep their eyes forward to avoid seeing dead bodies.

When the police arrived in Colin Goddard's classroom at Virginia Tech, "all I heard was, 'red tag, yellow tag, black tag, black tag, black tag,'" he said. "Yellow tag" indicated someone who was injured; "red tag" indicated someone who was severely injured; and "black tag" indicated someone who was dead. Police assigned Goddard a yellow tag, grabbed one of his arms, and pulled him from the classroom into the hallway. "The next thing I remember is I was then on my way to the hospital," said Goddard.

COMMON REACTIONS TO SCHOOL SHOOTINGS

Most people who survive a school shooting are traumatized by the event. They might be fine physically. Emotionally, however, they are a mess. ("We are OK, but no one is OK," was how Jordan Laudanno of Marjory Stoneman Douglas put it.) This is true whether a shooting involves large numbers of victims or just one. Even students whose schools are placed under lockdown due to a mere shooting *threat* may experience some degree of trauma. In one such case, a young student became so convinced he might die that he wrote a will and a heartbreaking goodbye letter. ("I love you my whole Family you mean the most to me," the boy wrote.)

Survivors of school shootings might also suffer trauma regardless of whether they were a direct victim of the shooting, witnessed it, were in or near the building when it occurred, or are members of the school community but were not present—although those who were physically closer to the event may be somewhat more affected. For some, the traumatic effect of the shooting is temporary. Others feel it forever.

In the aftermath of a school shooting, survivors might react to the trauma in different ways. Some might feel alienated from (or by) those who were not present for the attack because they do not understand what they're going through. This was true for Emily Mayberry of Northern Illinois University. Mayberry's boyfriend could not grasp why she was so disturbed by the shooting since she had not been in the room where it happened. ("Get over it!" he told her.) Shock, fear, anger, and sadness are other typical feelings among survivors after a school shooting.

Guilt is a very common reaction to a school shooting—particularly for school staff, but also for students. One form of guilt is survivor's guilt. This is when someone who experiences a traumatic event in which others die feels guilty or undeserving for surviving. In addition to survivor's guilt, some survivors feel guilty for failing to prevent the shooting. Others feel ashamed of their reaction during the shooting—for example, if they ran from the danger instead of staying behind to help others. This was true for one six-year-old student who survived a shooting on the playground at his school in Townville, South Carolina, in 2016. At the first sound of gunfire, the boy leaped over a fence and ran. A beloved friend, who stayed put, was killed in the shooting. "I should have waited for Jacob," the wrecked boy told his mother after the shooting.

Guilt also plagued Aalayah Eastmond at Marjory Stoneman Douglas after the shooting. When a classmate in front of her was killed by the gunman, Eastmond used the boy's body as a shield. That was how she survived. For her, the guilt eased only after she spoke to the boy's parents. "I thought they were going to be angry with me," she said. "But they

Parkland survivor Aalayah Eastmond speaks at the March for Our Lives.

weren't. They actually embraced me, and they were happy that I survived."

Some survivors don't feel shock, fear, anger, sadness, or guilt after a shooting. Instead, they feel … nothing. They go numb. That's what happened to Missy Dodds. Dodds was a math teacher at Red Lake

Sandy Hook Survivor Natalie Barden

As more school shootings occur, survivors have begun to speak out against gun violence. One such survivor is Natalie Barden. Barden was a fifth-grader at Sandy Hook Elementary School when a shooter murdered twenty children and six staff members. Natalie survived, but her little brother Daniel did not. Barden says that a long period of her life after Daniel's murder was a blur. She does remember her other brother and her "screaming and crying, both in the utmost pain imaginable, as our destroyed parents told us this news."

At first, after Daniel died, Barden just wanted to forget about the shooting. "All I wanted was to be normal and not constantly reminded of my loss," she says. But after the shooting at Marjory Stoneman Douglas High School in Parkland, Florida, everything changed. "I saw the teenagers down in Florida immediately speaking out for gun responsibility," Barden recalls. "It inspired me to do the same."

Natalie Barden and her mother on the one-month anniversary of the Sandy Hook Elementary School shooting

Now, Barden accepts requests for interviews about the shooting and attends meetings for a local gun-safety group. Barden also attended the March for Our Lives in Washington, DC, in March 2018. "This generation will enact change," Barden says. "We have no choice."

Senior High School in Minnesota when a student killed five classmates and two staff members in 2005. "You just shut down," Dodds said of her initial reaction to the event. "You have no feelings." For most, this numbness is temporary. And, "once the numbness wears off," said Dodds, "the pain is intolerable."

PSYCHOLOGICAL EFFECTS OF SCHOOL SHOOTINGS

It's not unusual or surprising for survivors of a school shooting to experience ongoing psychological effects. This is particularly true of children and adolescents. This is because violent events like school shootings can alter the shape of their brain. The result is often ongoing problems like attention deficit disorder, numbness to violence, anxiety, problems sleeping, and more.

Post-traumatic stress syndrome (PTSD) affects many survivors of school shootings. People with this condition have intrusive memories, flashbacks, nightmares, panic attacks, and negative changes in thinking and mood. These might include:

- Negative thoughts about yourself, others, or the world

- a general sense of hopelessness

- a feeling of detachment

- a sense of alienation, even from close friends and family

People with PTSD might also be easily startled or frightened—for example, if a car backfires or someone sets off fireworks—constantly on guard, irritable, or unable to concentrate.

Speaking of concentrating: according to a report shared by a gun-safety organization called Everytown for Gun Safety, "violence in schools may hinder students from learning efficiently." In fact, "standardized test scores in math and English are lower in affected schools for up to three years after a deadly shooting." This may have a long-term impact on students. For example, if they score lower on tests, they might not be able to get into more selective colleges. This could in turn affect how much money they earn when they enter the workforce.

Columbine shooting victim Austin Eubanks with his girlfriend in the aftermath of the attack

For some survivors of school shootings, the psychological effects are long-lasting. According to the Everytown report, adolescent victims of violence such as school shootings are "more likely to experience depression as an adult." Adult survivors of school shootings may also have nightmares and flashbacks when they see news of another school shooting.

Some survivors of school shootings try to "medicate" their psychological pain by turning to alcohol or drugs. That was true for Columbine survivor Austin Eubanks. Eubanks suffered two gunshot wounds in the attack, and his best friend was killed. When doctors gave Eubanks pain relievers to ease his physical pain, he found that the drugs also "took the emotion away." Within a matter of weeks, he was hooked on painkillers. For Eubanks, abusing drugs was a way to avoid dealing with his grief. (Eubanks later became sober and now helps others who suffer from drug addiction.)

The Copycat Effect

News vans gather at Virginia Tech University after the mass shooting there. Media coverage of school shootings could inspire copycat violence.

School shootings get a lot of attention in the news—particularly rampages. The students who commit these shootings often become quite famous. Unfortunately, this may inspire other shooters to act— a phenomenon called copycat violence.

To prevent copycat violence, gun-safety organizations have pushed media outlets to change how they cover school shootings. So far this has not worked. Members of the media generally feel that reporting detailed information about school shooters is part of their job. They also believe it informs the debate on the issue of school shootings.

One gun-safety organization called the Brady Campaign has attacked the problem from a different angle. They developed a plug-in for the Google Chrome web browser that censors the names of mass shooters in internet news stories "out of respect for the victims." The Brady Campaign has also released a public service announcement on the issue and circulated an online petition to encourage change in the media coverage of school shootings. These efforts are mostly symbolic but still powerful.

Chapter 4

Hope and Recovery

Recovering from a school shooting is a slow and painful process. Fortunately, there are several steps that survivors can take to heal. It's important to focus on both physical and mental health in the period after a school shooting. This means eating well-balanced meals, getting regular exercise, and getting plenty of sleep. (If a survivor is suffering from insomnia, relaxation techniques such as deep breathing, meditation, or yoga can help.)

Opposite: Recovering from a tramautic event like a school shooting is difficult, but there is hope.

STEPS TO RECOVERY

Of course, for survivors who are injured during a school shooting, restoring their physical health is most important. This may mean undergoing surgeries or rehabilitation.

Often, restoring physical health is simpler than regaining mental health. For many survivors of school shootings, talking to a psychotherapist was what helped them the most in this aspect of their recovery. This was particularly true for survivors who developed post-traumatic stress syndrome (PTSD) after the shooting.

Psychotherapists use different approaches to treat survivors with PTSD. The most common approach is talk therapy. Talk therapy means talking one-on-one with a psychotherapist. It could also mean participating in group sessions with others who suffer from a similar diagnosis. Another approach is eye movement desensitization and reprocessing (EMDR) therapy. According to the World Health Organization,

EMDR involves working through trauma while making certain eye or hand movements. This helps the patient process negative memories and causes thoughts, feelings, or behaviors connected to that memory to fall away. (Some people don't believe EMDR works. Many patients report good results, however.) In addition to these and other forms of therapy, a psychotherapist might prescribe medication to restore the chemical balance of the brain.

Seeking support from fellow victims of school shootings may help survivors restore their mental health. This might mean checking in with people who experienced the same shooting they did or connecting with survivors of other shootings. Both may help survivors feel less alienated and alone. Plus, talking with fellow survivors may have another positive consequence: you may help them. And of course, survivors should talk with family and friends. Some survivors might be tempted to bottle up their feelings. Maybe sharing them is painful, or maybe

Stages of Grief

Elisabeth Kübler-Ross

Many people who experience a traumatic event such as a school shooting feel grief. Often this grief occurs in stages.

Psychiatrist Elisabeth Kübler-Ross identified five stages of grief. The first stage of grief is denial. During this stage, survivors deny their feelings about the event. As denial fades, anger often kicks in. This is the second stage of grief. Anger often returns the survivor to reality. The third stage is bargaining. During this stage, survivors fixate on *ifs* and *if onlys*. They think a lot about turning back time. The fourth stage is depression. During this stage, the survivor might withdraw or even think about dying by suicide. The fifth and final stage of grief is acceptance. In this stage, survivors accept what happened. This does not mean they are OK with what took place. It just means they understand that they must live with it.

Not everyone experiences all these stages of grief or goes through them in this order. Sometimes, survivors circle back and repeat stages before finally gaining acceptance. This may take time. Regardless of where survivors are in this process, they should honor their feelings and give themselves time to experience them.

they are afraid others don't want to hear about them. But this can prolong the healing process or stall it completely.

To maintain their mental health, survivors might want to take a break from (or at least limit their exposure to) the news after a school shooting. The American Psychological Association (APA) explains why: "Being overexposed to [the news] can actually increase your stress. The images can be very powerful in reawakening your feeling of distress." On a related note, the APA suggests scheduling time to focus on things you enjoy.

Often, survivors of a school shooting feel overwhelmed by negative feelings during the recovery phase. When that happens, it might be soothing to remember this famous quote from Fred Rogers, who was the host of the popular children's show *Mr. Rogers' Neighborhood*: "When I was a boy and I would see scary things in the news, my mother would say to me, 'Look for the helpers. You will always find people who are helping.'"

Teachers Jenny Darnall and Kelly Weaver emphasized this lesson after a student gunned down two classmates and wounded fourteen others at Marshall County High School in Benton, Kentucky, in 2018. "Look at the banners and letters and cards pouring in from across the country," they told students. "Look at the comfort dogs and comfort food. See the fellowship in it."

Makeshift memorials, like this one in honor of those killed at Virginia Tech, can help comfort survivors.

Survivor Hotlines and Support Organizations

Telephone hotlines can help victims of violence.

While there are no hotlines geared specifically toward survivors of school shootings, there are general hotlines for victims of trauma. These include the following:

The Disaster Distress Hotline: 1-800-985-5990

The National Alliance on Mental Illness (NAMI) Hotline: 1-800-950-NAMI

Survivors of school violence can also reach out to organizations that assist victims of school shootings and other forms of gun violence online. Some of these organizations were founded by survivors or by families of people killed by gun violence. These organizations can help survivors connect with others who have suffered similar ordeals or channel their energies toward reducing gun violence. Here are just a few:

Everytown Survivor Network: https://everytown.org/survivors

The Rebels Project: http://therebelsproject.org

Survivors Empowered: https://www.survivorsempowered.org

With time, some survivors of school shootings might see a silver lining of sorts. Of course, they will never be glad it happened. But they might feel that some good came out of it. That was true for Emily Mayberry of Northern Illinois University. "Being so close to death made me realize my mortality," she said later. "It made me want to go for things instead of holding back in fear." Colin Goddard, who was shot at Virginia Tech, had a similar reaction. "I was a struggling student before the shooting," he said. "The shooting really straightened me out in that sense." When Goddard healed from his wounds and returned to school, "I did better than I ever did before."

Even if survivors can't see a silver lining in their experience, they might at least manage to live in such a way that the experience doesn't define them. That was the experience of Nicolle Martin, who survived the shooting at Marjory Stoneman Douglas. "There's no undoing the pain of the Parkland massacre," Martin wrote. "But it won't define me or my school."

SURVIVOR ACTIVISM

Some survivors of school shootings—as well as students who are simply concerned about gun violence—channel their pain and gain strength by engaging in activism to end gun violence. This activism takes many forms.

For some survivors, activism is about writing articles for newspapers or doing interviews on TV to discuss their experiences or to push for change. Brooke Harrison of Marjory Stoneman Douglas and Natalie Barden of Sandy Hook have engaged in this kind of activism. These students wrote moving articles for ABC News and *Teen Vogue*, respectively.

Another form of survivor activism is marching. For example, survivors of the shooting at Marjory Stoneman Douglas, along with other young activists around the country, organized the March for Our Lives in March 2018. The march occurred in Washington, DC, with satellite marches in other cities around the country.

Students at Marjory Stoneman Douglas also staged a walkout to demand change. They were joined in this by students nationwide. According to the *New York Times*:

In New York City, in Chicago, in Atlanta and Santa Monica; at Columbine High School and in Newtown, Conn.; and in many more cities and towns, students left school by the hundreds and the thousands at 10:00 a.m., sometimes in defiance of school authorities, who seemed divided and even flummoxed about how to handle their emptying classrooms.

In another walkout, in Baltimore, Maryland, students didn't just walk out of school. They issued a list of demands. These included:

- A ban on lethal weapons in educational institutions

- Putting social workers and counselors in schools

- Passing a bill to ban detachable magazines capable of holding more than ten rounds of ammunition

- Passing a bill to allow law enforcement officials to temporarily take guns from people who pose a threat to themselves or others

They also followed a strict code of conduct that included walking only on sidewalks, cooperating with police, and practicing nonviolence.

In 2018, students across the country staged walkouts to protest gun violence and push for change.

Not everyone thinks students should engage in activism—particularly walkouts. Some schools have punished students who organize walkouts or other protests. It's important that students know their school's rules with regard to protests. But they should also understand their rights. For example, although schools are free to punish students for their unexcused absence during a walkout, they are *not* allowed to issue a punishment that is more severe than for other unexcused absences. Nor can schools lock exits to prevent a walkout.

GETTING INVOLVED: HOW YOU CAN HELP

Two days after the tragic shooting at Sandy Hook Elementary School in Newtown, Connecticut, President Barack Obama delivered these moving words during a prayer vigil:

> We cannot tolerate this anymore. These tragedies must end. And to end them, we must change. We will be told that the

causes of such violence are complex, and that is true. No single law—no set of laws can eliminate evil from the world, or prevent every senseless act of violence in our society. But that cannot be an excuse for inaction. Surely, we can do better than this. If there is even one step we can take to save another child, or another parent, or another town ... then surely we have an obligation to try.

Students who interpret President Obama's words as a call to action can get involved in the fight to prevent school shootings and other forms of gun violence. One way to do so is to ally yourself with an organization devoted to this cause—particularly one geared toward young people.

One such organization is Students Against Violence Everywhere (SAVE) (http://nationalsave .org), which merged with another gun-safety group, called Sandy Hook Promise, in 2017. Thousands of schools and youth groups nationwide have SAVE chapters, called SAVE Promise clubs. These clubs

President Obama at the Sandy Hook vigil in December 2012

teach nonviolence, civility, and conflict-management skills. They also teach ways for young people to prevent crime and generally be good citizens. If your school does not have a SAVE Promise club you can start your own. For more information, visit https://www.sandyhookpromise.org/savepromiseclub.

March for Our Lives (https://marchforourlives.com) is another youth-oriented gun-safety group. It was founded in 2018 by Parkland shooting survivors and other young activists from around the country. March for Our Lives has quickly grown to include millions of members, young and old, who seek to end gun violence. As with SAVE Promise clubs, students can join an existing March for Our Lives chapter or start their own. For more details, see https://marchforourlives.com/local-action.

While other gun-safety organizations aren't geared toward young people, they still welcome youth involvement. These include:

- Sandy Hook Promise (https://www.sandyhookpromise.org)

- Giffords Law Center to Prevent Gun Violence (https://lawcenter.giffords.org)

- Everytown for Gun Safety (https://everytown.org)

- The Brady Campaign to Prevent Gun Violence (http://www.bradycampaign.org)

Another way to get involved is to engage in the political process. That means writing or calling your federal, state, and local representatives to tell them

After a Shooting: How Schools Can Help

School counselors can help students heal in the aftermath of a school shooting.

After a shooting, schools should work to restore a routine as quickly as possible— even if this routine is different from the old one. Unfortunately, there's no manual for achieving this. "How each school community responds to these tragedies is based largely on their established climate and culture and how quickly the members of the school community can bond, grieve, and begin the healing process," says Principal George Roberts of Perry Hall High near Baltimore, Maryland. (In 2012, a gunman injured one Perry Hall student.)

One proven way to kick-start this return to routine is to convene a special assembly on everyone's first day back. During this assembly, school officials can discuss the shooting, explain any new security efforts enacted as a result of the attack, and relay what help is available for students and staff suffering psychological effects in the aftermath of the shooting. (Schools should keep grief counselors who specialize in crisis intervention on site for at least a month after the incident.)

For additional guidance, school administrators can contact the National Center for School Crisis and Bereavement (NCSCB). The NCSCB has helped thousands of schools and communities cope after a crisis, including school shootings. For more information, see https://www.schoolcrisiscenter.org.

your views on gun violence—not just once, but often. (To find out who your representatives are, and how to contact them, visit https://www.commoncause .org, click Find Your Representatives, and enter your address.) If you're old enough, it also means registering to vote and voting in all elections.

Helping victims and families is yet another way to stay active. If a shooting happens at your school or in your community, stay alert to ways you can help survivors. If a shooting takes place in another city or state, you can help by donating to online fundraisers that have been set up for victims and their families (or by setting up a fundraiser yourself).

Finally, you can help by keeping the conversation going. All too often, school shootings and gun violence become hot topics in the immediate aftermath of an attack, but slowly fade as new stories enter the news cycle. Don't let that happen! Keep talking and keep fighting for an end to gun violence.

Glossary

activist Someone who takes vigorous action for or against one side of a controversial issue.

copycat violence A phenomenon in which the attention received by one school shooter (or other violent person) inspires another school shooter (or violent person) to act.

emasculate To diminish someone's masculinity or manhood.

handgun A gun designed to be fired with one hand.

lockdown When a school or other building locks all its doors and refuses to let anyone in or out as a protective measure against some type of threat.

Machiavellian Describes someone who seeks power by any means necessary, including manipulation and even violence.

magazine A container in or on a firearm that feeds bullets into the gun's chamber.

manifesto An explanation of someone's views or motives.

narcissist Someone with excessive self-esteem. Narcissists feel entitled to extra attention and special treatment, and they lash out when they don't get it.

pistol A type of handgun.

profiling The act of suspecting someone of something or targeting someone based on specific traits or behaviors.

psychopath Someone who disregards and even violates the rights of others in the pursuit of their goals. Some psychopaths do not view other people as human beings.

rifle A long gun.

schizophrenic Someone who suffers from schizophrenia, which is a mental illness characterized by disturbances in thought, perception, and behavior.

school rampage A random school shooting involving four or more victims and at least two deaths.

school shooting An incident in which someone fires a gun on school grounds during school hours while students are on site.

semiautomatic Describes a gun that is reloaded automatically but that requires the user to pull the trigger for each shot (rather than simply holding it down).

survivor's guilt When someone who survives a traumatic event in which others die feels guilty or undeserving for surviving.

tourniquet A medical device that helps stop excessive bleeding by compressing the blood vessels.

walkout A form of protest that involves "walking out" of a school, place of business, or other organization.

Further Information

BOOKS

The Founders of March for Our Lives. *Glimmer of Hope: How Tragedy Sparked a Movement.* New York: Razorbill, 2018.

Marsico, Katie. *The Columbine High School Massacre: Murder in the Classroom.* New York: Benchmark Books, 2010.

Steele, Philip. *Behind the News: School Shootings.* London, UK: Wayland Publishers, 2018.

WEBSITES

K–12 School Shooting Database

https://www.chds.us/ssdb

Hosted by the Center for Homeland Defense and Security, this database tracks school shootings and is updated regularly.

Ready: Active Shooter

https://www.ready.gov/active-shooter

Explore tips for surviving a school shooting and read about how to make a plan.

StopBullying.gov

https://www.stopbullying.gov

This site provides tips to prevent bullying, which is thought to be a contributor to school shootings.

VIDEOS

RUN. HIDE. FIGHT. Surviving an Active Shooter Event

https://www.youtube.com/
watch?v=5VcSwejU2D0&feature=player_embedded

The City of Houston produced this video about preparing for an active shooter.

Students Demonstrate How to Survive a School Shooting

https://www.teenvogue.com/story/what-to-do-in-school-shooting-video

Five student activists show you how to survive a school shooting.

Bibliography

Barden, Natalie. "Natalie Barden Refllects on the Sandy Hook Shooting, the March for Our Lives, and Why She Still Fights for Gun-Violence Prevention." *Teen Vogue*, August 15, 2018. https://www.teenvogue.com/story/natalie-barden-sandy-hook-march-for-our-lives-gun-violence-op-ed?verso=true.

Bushman, Brad J., Sandra L. Calvert, Mark Dredze, Nina G. Jablonski, Calvin Morrill, Daniel Romer, Katherine Newman, et al. "Youth Violence: What We Know and What We Need to Know." *American Psychologist* 71(1): 17–39. https://www.apa.org/pubs/journals/releases/amp-a0039687.pdf.

Cox, John Woodrow, Steven Rich, Allyson Chiu, John Muyskens, and Monica Ulmanu. "More Than 215,000 Students Have Experienced Gun Violence at School Since Columbine." *Washington Post*, October 2, 2018. https://www.washingtonpost.com/graphics/2018/local/school-shootings-database/?utm_term=.bb91647c5280.

Harrison, Brooke. "Parkland Shooting Survivor Pens Personal Account, 'We Were Children That Came Out as Survivors